WILLOW DISCOVERS WELDING

Inspired by a true story.

EDITED BY CAYCE FINLEY
ILLUSTRATIONS BY MONIQUE RENEE

Written and designed by Kelli Gilliam.

Thank you
to my husband, Sheldon,
my kids, Ethan, Aaron, Laila, Sofia, Delilah,
my father, William Royals,
and all those who have supported me.

A Special Thank you to
Nherie Tellado, Janelle Roberts, Diana Morris,
Carley Ferrara, Hailee Manipole, Nicholas Morris
your donations contribute to
"Changing the Perspective of Manufacturing".

I love to swing outside.
Sometimes when I swing, I think.
Today I wondered where
I would work when I get older.

Later that day, my mom and I sat at the table. I did my homework. She was dressed funny. "What is your job?" I asked in between math problems.

"I am a welder. I connect the big parts of a ship together," mom answered.
"Can you teach me to weld," I asked.
Mom said, "Of course!"

"Can welding hurt me?" I asked Mom.
She smiled. "Remember when we baked a pie and
had to wear special mittens to
protect our hands from the hot oven?
It's like that," she said.

The next day, I could not wait to
get home from school.
Mom was finishing a welding project.
She said I could help!

Mom had everything ready.
I spotted gloves that looked like baking mitts
and a big mask that looked like a robot.
"Just like sunglasses protect your eyes
from the sun, the mask protects your eyes
from the welding light," Mom explained.

"Do you like to weld, Mom?" I asked later that night.

"Willow, welding is like going to
art class everyday!" she said with a grin.

"Do you think I can be a welder like you?" I asked softly.

"You can be anything you want!" Mom answered.

The next week, Mom greeted me with a huge smile
as I came in the door.
"Willow, it's family day at my work tomorrow.
Would you like to come?" she asked.
"Yes!" I said, jumping up and down.

That afternoon, as I sat on my swing, I thought
about all the exciting things I would see.

This book is dedicated to my five children:
Ethan, Aaron, Laila, Sofia, Delilah and in
memory of my mother who taught me how to
be a mother by her life example. You are
forever with us.

Gloria Jean Royals

Oct.1954-Mar.2019

CPSIA information can be obtained
at www.ICGtesting.com
Printed in the USA
BVRC101159100821
614091BV00011B/695